On Dreams

Aristotle's Philosophical and Scientific Inquiry into Dreaming

A Modern Translation

Adapted for the Contemporary Reader

Aristotle

Table of Contents

Preface - Message to the Reader

Rebuilding the Greatest Library in Human History

Thousands of years ago, the Library of Alexandria was the heart of global knowledge — a sanctuary where the wisdom of every known civilization was gathered and shared freely.

And then, it was lost.

Now, we're rebuilding it — and you are invited to join us.

At the Library of Alexandria, we've set out to make every book available to *every person on Earth* — not just in print, but in every language, every format, and for every reader.

Here's how we do it:

- **Deluxe Print Editions at True Printing Cost** - Order any book as a high-quality paperback, elegant hardcover, or stunning boxset — and only pay what it costs to print. No markups. No middlemen.

- **Unlimited Access to the Greatest Works** - Enjoy thousands of timeless classics — from Plato to Shakespeare to Tolstoy — in beautiful, modern eBook and audiobook editions. Read and listen without limits — for every reader, everywhere.

- **Modern Translations for Every Language & Dialect** - We're reimagining the classics in clear, accessible language — and translating them into every dialect imaginable. Everyone deserves to understand humanity's greatest ideas.

When you visit **LibraryofAlexandria.com**, you're not just accessing books — you're joining a global movement to restore, preserve, and share the wisdom of civilization.

Join us today at LibraryofAlexandria.com

Together, we'll ensure the light of human wisdom never fades again.

With gratitude,
The Modern Library of Alexandria Team

Visit:

www.libraryofalexandria.com

Or scan the code below:

Introduction

Ancient Greece was a civilization famous for its great contributions to philosophy, politics, art, and science. It thrived from the 8th century BCE until the Roman Empire started to decline. Greece's city-states, especially Athens, were the heart of culture and intellectual thought. This was the time when democracy began, impressive buildings like the Parthenon were built, and famous playwrights like Sophocles and Euripides produced their works. The Greeks' curiosity about the world around them laid the foundation for Western philosophy. Thinkers like Socrates, Plato, and later Aristotle, pushed the limits of what people understood about the world.

Greek society was deeply connected to theism, which focused on a large group of gods and goddesses who were believed to control every part of life. But this system did not prevent people from exploring new ideas. In fact, it coexisted with a growing interest in finding logical explanations for nature and human life. Intellectuals would often debate and discuss these ideas in public places like the Agora. Aristotle grew up in this dynamic environment, learning from earlier philosophers, and later challenging and expanding their ideas.

Aristotle's Life

Aristotle was born in 384 BCE in a small town called Stagira, located in northern Greece. His father, Nicomachus, was a doctor for King Amyntas of Macedon, and this allowed Aristotle to be around the Macedonian royal court from a young age. When his parents passed away, Aristotle was sent to Athens at the age of 17 to pursue his education. Athens was the center of intellectual life in Greece, and Aristotle joined Plato's Academy, which was the most respected school of the time. The Academy was a place where students discussed everything from ethics to science. Although Aristotle learned a lot from Plato, he did not always agree with him, especially when it came to metaphysics, which deals with the nature of reality.

After spending almost 20 years at the Academy, Aristotle left Athens around 347 BCE after Plato's death. He traveled around different cities in Greece, continuing to study and learn. In 343 BCE, he was invited to the court of King Philip II of Macedon, where he became the tutor of Philip's son, Alexander, who would later become known as Alexander the Great. Aristotle taught Alexander about philosophy, ethics, politics, and science. Aristotle's influence is visible in Alexander's leadership style, which showed respect for knowledge and strategic thinking.

After teaching Alexander, Aristotle returned to Athens in 335 BCE, where he opened his own school called the Lyceum. Unlike Plato's Academy, the Lyceum focused more on recording knowledge and observing nature. Aristotle and his students performed research, studied animals, and took notes on what they observed. The Lyceum became a major center of learning, and it rivaled Plato's Academy. This is also where Aristotle wrote many of his famous works.

Later in life, after the death of Alexander in 323 BCE, the political climate in Athens became difficult for Aristotle because of his connections to the Macedonian court. Accused of disrespecting the gods, Aristotle decided to leave Athens. He fled to Chalcis, where he passed away in 322 BCE. Even though he had to leave Athens, his legacy lived on through his many writings and the influence of his school, the Lyceum.

Aristotle's Impact on Western Thought

No figure looms larger over the development of Western philosophy and science than Aristotle. A student of Plato and tutor to Alexander the Great, he unified logic, ethics, politics, rhetoric, and metaphysics into a coherent system that shaped intellectual inquiry for centuries. Although his writings reflect the best knowledge of his era, they also reveal a distinctive way of understanding the world—one that balances observation with rigorous logical analysis. Over time, this method has profoundly influenced everything from political theory to modern scientific methodology.

Aristotle approached knowledge as an interconnected whole, seeing each field of study as a vital path toward truth. While many earlier thinkers focused on abstract concepts, he emphasized direct observation of the natural world. By systematically examining and classifying what he saw, Aristotle laid the groundwork for the empirical methods now central to modern science. Although our understanding of nature has evolved, his legacy endures in today's emphasis on evidence-based research.

Logic: The Foundation of Rational Inquiry

Often hailed as the "father of formal logic," Aristotle introduced a system of reasoning that shaped intellectual discourse for over two millennia. In works like the Organon, he analyzed how valid conclusions are drawn from premises and introduced syllogisms—deductive arguments that became standard tools in philosophy, theology, and science. Even contemporary logic, despite its modern mathematical and symbolic advancements, can trace many of its core principles back to Aristotle's pioneering analyses.

Metaphysics: Exploring the Nature of Reality

Aristotle's Metaphysics offered one of the earliest comprehensive explorations of existence at its most fundamental level. There, he described the nature of "being qua being" and introduced the concepts of potentiality and actuality to explain how things change and develop. These ideas deeply influenced medieval scholastics—both Christian and Islamic—who integrated Aristotelian reasoning into their theological frameworks. Today, discussions about consciousness, identity, and free will still reference these Aristotelian notions.

Ethics and the Pursuit of the Good Life

In the Nicomachean Ethics, Aristotle proposed that the ultimate aim of human life is eudaimonia, often translated as "happiness" or "flourishing." He argued that we achieve this through virtue, developed by cultivating good habits guided by reason. His famous Doctrine of the Mean asserts that moral virtue resides between two extremes—for instance, courage lies between recklessness and cowardice. This focus on character formation has profoundly shaped the tradition known as "virtue ethics," influencing modern debates on moral education, personal development, and what it means to live well.

Politics: The Role of the Individual in the City-State

Aristotle's practical approach to ethics naturally extended into political theory. In Politics, he explored various forms of government—monarchy, aristocracy, oligarchy, democracy—and weighed their merits and pitfalls. For Aristotle, a well-ordered polis (city-state) exists not merely for survival or trade but to enable its citizens to live virtuous, fulfilling lives. His conviction that ethics and politics are intertwined remains influential, informing contemporary discussions on citizenship, governance, and justice.

Rhetoric: The Art of Persuasion

In his treatise Rhetoric, Aristotle examined how persuasion works, detailing how arguments must appeal to ethos (credibility), pathos (emotion), and logos (logic). This clear framework for effective communication continues to guide public speakers, legal advocates, and writers. From ancient courtroom orations to modern political campaigns, Aristotelian rhetoric underpins many of the strategies people use to sway audiences and shape public opinion.

Beyond these core subjects, Aristotle made significant contributions to biology, physics, psychology, and aesthetics. In the Poetics, for example, he investigated why humans respond so powerfully to tragic drama, pioneering the concept of catharsis— the emotional release that audiences feel through art. Throughout the medieval period, thinkers like Thomas Aquinas integrated Aristotle's theories into Christian theology, while Islamic philosophers such as Avicenna and Averroes preserved, interpreted, and expanded upon his works.

Across centuries of reinterpretation and debate, Aristotle remains a living voice in contemporary thought. His insistence on systematically gathering evidence and connecting it to logical principles laid the foundation for what we now recognize as the scientific method. His inquiries into human flourishing, civic responsibility, and the nature of argument continue to spark discussion and inspire new research. From personal ethics to societal organization, Aristotle's ideas help us frame enduring questions about how best to live, learn, and understand reality.

In sum, Aristotle stands as a foundational pillar of Western thought. He bridged abstract theorizing and practical inquiry, bequeathing a vision of knowledge that values both reason and experience. From ethics and politics to science and art, his ideas have been woven into countless intellectual traditions. Even today, as we grapple with questions of morality, governance, and truth, we walk in the footsteps of an ancient thinker whose breadth of insight and depth of analysis continue to guide our pursuit of wisdom.

Final Thoughts

By preserving Aristotle's legacy, we protect the intellectual depth and rigor that defined his way of understanding the world. His systematic way of asking questions, his classification of knowledge, and his ethical theories are still relevant today, providing a model for critical thinking across many subjects. This preservation is important not just for philosophy students but for anyone interested in the foundations of human thought and the development of ideas that shape the world we live in.

One of the difficulties in studying Aristotle's work is that his ideas and language are complex. Translating these works into our modern language is a key step in making his profound insights easier for more people to understand. By putting his ideas into today's language, more readers can engage with his thoughts, even if they don't have a background in classical studies. Making Aristotle's work accessible means adapting them to modern ways of thinking without losing their original depth. This helps bridge the gap between ancient and modern readers, making sure Aristotle's work stays relevant.

On Dreams

Next, we need to explore the topic of dreams and first figure out which part of the soul is responsible for dreams—whether they come from the part that thinks or the part that senses, since these are the only ways we gain knowledge.

If using the eyes means seeing, using the ears means hearing, and using our senses means perceiving, and if there are things that all senses can detect, like shape, size, and motion, while other things like color, sound, and taste are specific to each sense, then it's clear that when animals close their eyes to sleep, they can't see anymore. The same applies to other senses. This shows that when we are asleep, we don't sense anything, so it can't be through sense-perception that we experience dreams.

But dreams don't come from opinion either. For example, in a dream, we might think a shape approaching us is a man or a horse, which would be forming an opinion, but we also think the figure is white or beautiful. However, we don't form opinions about things like color or beauty without using our senses. Even so, in dreams, we make such judgments. In a dream, we seem to see both the figure of the person and the fact that the person is white. Sometimes, while dreaming, we think about more than just the dream itself, just like we do when we are awake and sense something. We often reason about what we see. In the same way, while asleep, we sometimes think about things beyond the dream images in front of us. Anyone who tries to remember their dreams right after waking up would notice this. Some people dream about organizing things in their mind according to a memory rule, for example. They often find themselves doing more than just dreaming—they also work on placing the dream images into memory. So, it's clear that not every image in a dream is just a simple dream, and that the extra thinking we do is related to opinion.

At least, it's clear that the part of us responsible for illusions while awake—like when we are sick—is the same part that causes us to have illusions while we sleep. Even when people are healthy and know what's true, the sun still looks like it's only a foot wide. Whether the part of the soul responsible for creating images is the same or different from the part that senses things, illusions can't happen without actually seeing or perceiving something. Even seeing or hearing something incorrectly only happens if we are actually seeing or hearing something, even if it's not what we think it is. But in sleep, we don't see or hear or sense anything real. So, maybe it's true that we don't actually see anything in dreams, but that doesn't mean the senses aren't involved at all. It's possible that our senses are affected in some way during sleep, and that this affects the main sense organ, though not exactly in the same way it does when we are awake. Sometimes, even in dreams, our opinion tells us that what we are seeing isn't real, just like it does when we are awake. Other times, it follows the dream image without questioning it.

So, it's clear that dreaming isn't simply a matter of opinion or reasoning, but it's also not just a simple function of the senses. If it were only about the senses, we would be able to hear and see things in our dreams in the same way we do when we are awake.

Now we need to figure out how dreaming happens and what exactly it is. Let's assume something that's pretty clear: dreaming is related to sense-perception in the same way that sleep is. After all, sleep and dreaming don't involve different organs; both come from the same part.

Since we've already discussed in another work that creating mental images is related to sense-perception, and the ability to create images is the same as the ability to sense things (though thinking about images is different from simply sensing things), and since images come from the activity of the senses, and dreams seem to be images, it's clear that dreaming involves sense-perception, but in a way that's connected to creating images.

We can understand dreams better by looking at what happens during sleep. When we sense something, whether it's through seeing, hearing, or any other sense, the object of that sense leaves an impression on our senses. These impressions stay with us even after the object is gone.

This is like how a moving object, like a rock, keeps moving even after the thing that set it in motion stops touching it. The rock moves through the air because it pushed the air in front of it, and that air pushes the air in front of it, continuing the motion until the rock stops. The same thing happens when something causes a change in quality, like heat. If one part of something gets hot, it heats up the part next to it, and the heat spreads until the whole thing is warm. The same process happens in our sense organs. When we sense something, the sensory change continues in our organs even after the object we were sensing is gone.

This is easy to see when we focus on a particular sense for a long time. If we stare at something bright and then look at darkness, we won't see anything for a while because the light left an impression in our eyes. If we stare at a bright color like white or green, the next thing we look at will seem to have that color. If we look at the sun or something else bright and then close our eyes, we'll still see the image of the sun for a while, first in its own color, then in red, purple, and finally black before it disappears. The same thing happens if we watch something moving, like a fast-flowing river, and then look away. The still objects around us will seem to move because the impression of movement is still in our eyes. People's hearing gets worse after listening to loud sounds, and after smelling strong odors, our sense of smell is weaker. The same thing happens with all the other senses.

Our sense organs are sensitive to even small changes, as we can see by looking at mirrors. Mirrors deserve to be studied closely on their own, but they also show that just as the eyes are affected by what they see, they also affect what they look at. If a woman looks into a polished mirror while she's on her period, the surface of the mirror can become cloudy, with a reddish tint. It's hard to remove this stain from a new mirror, but easier from an old one. The reason this happens is that when we see something, the sense organ is affected by the object, but it also has an effect on the object, especially if the object is bright. Seeing involves brightness and color, and the eyes, like other body parts, have their own effects. Because the eyes are full of blood vessels, a woman's eyes change when she's on her period, but her husband won't notice this because his body is similar to hers. The air around the mirror and the person looking into it also changes, which causes the mirror's surface to be affected. Just like a clean garment gets dirty quickly, a clean mirror shows even small stains clearly. A shiny bronze mirror, for example, is especially sensitive to contact because the air around it acts like it's rubbing or pressing against it. That's why clean mirrors show even the smallest smudges. It's hard to clean a new mirror because the stain goes deep, but old mirrors don't hold stains as easily because the stains only affect the surface.

So, it's clear that even small changes can cause movements in the senses and that our sense organs respond quickly to them. It's also clear that the organ responsible for seeing color isn't just affected by the color but also affects it. We can see the same thing in how oil and wine are affected by the smells around them. Oil and wine take on the smells of things nearby, not just what's mixed with them, but also things that are close to them or grow near them.

To answer the question we started with, let's assume a few things that we know are true: even after the thing we were sensing is gone, the impression it left behind stays with us, and we can still sense it. Also, we are easily fooled by our senses when we're emotional, and different people are affected by different emotions. For example, a scared person might think they see an enemy, and a person in love might think they see the object of their desire, even if there's only a slight resemblance. The more emotional we are, the less it takes for us to be tricked by our senses. This is why people who have fevers sometimes think they see animals on the walls. The markings on the walls might look like animals, and this illusion gets stronger if the person's emotions are high. If the illness isn't too bad, they can still tell it's not real, but if they're very sick, they might start reacting to what they think they see. The reason this happens is that the part of us that judges what we see isn't the same as the part that presents the images to us. We can see this in how the sun looks small even though we know it's big. When we cross our fingers and touch something, it feels like we're touching two things instead of one, but we know there's only one because our sight is more reliable than touch. If we only relied on touch, we would believe there were two things. These false judgments happen because we can have perceptions even when the sense isn't directly interacting with the object. For example, people on a moving ship might think the land is moving when really, it's their eyes that are being moved by the ship.

It's clear from this that the movements caused by sensory impressions, whether they come from things outside the body or from within, happen not only when people are awake but even more strongly when they are asleep. During the day, when the senses and the mind are working together, these movements are pushed aside or hidden, like a small fire next to a larger one, or a small pain or pleasure compared to a greater one. When the bigger one fades, we notice the smaller one. But at night, when we sleep, because the senses are inactive and can't work properly, the movements are sent to the main center of sense-perception and show themselves once the activity of being awake fades away. We can think of these movements like small whirlpools in a river, which keep going, sometimes staying as they were when they started, but other times getting broken up by obstacles.

This explains why we don't dream right after eating or why young children, like infants, don't dream. The internal movement in these cases is too strong because of the heat generated by food. Just like in water, if it's stirred up too much, sometimes no reflection appears, or if it does, it looks distorted, not like the original image. But once the water calms down, the reflection becomes clear. In the same way, during sleep, the movements left over from sensory impressions are sometimes wiped out by this strong movement. Other times, the images are there, but they're confused and strange. The dreams that come at these times are unhealthy, like the dreams of people who are sick, have too much bile, or are drunk. All these conditions create a lot of disturbance and unrest in the body. In animals with blood, when the blood calms down and its pure parts are separated from the impure ones, the movements left from the senses remain clear, and the dreams are healthy. The dreamer then believes they are actually seeing something because of the movements coming from the sense of sight, or hearing something because of the movements coming from the sense of hearing, and so on for the other senses. It's because these movements come from the senses that we sometimes believe we are seeing, hearing, or feeling something, even when we're awake. For example, sometimes we mistakenly think we see something when the eye is not really being stimulated, or think one object is two because of the way our sense of touch is sending signals. Usually, our main sense organ accepts what each particular sense reports, unless another sense contradicts it.

In every case, something appears, but what appears doesn't always seem real unless the main sense organ is blocked or not working properly. Just as different people are fooled by different emotions when they are awake, the same happens in sleep. The sleeper, because of the movements in their senses during sleep, as well as the other sensory processes, is easily fooled. So, a dream, even if it's not exactly like reality, seems like a real thing. When we sleep, most of the blood moves inward toward the heart, and the sensory movements, some potential and some active, move inward with it. They are related to each other in such a way that if the blood is moved, one sensory movement will show up, and if that one disappears, another will take its place. They are like toy frogs in water, which rise to the surface one by one as the salt holding them down dissolves. The remaining sensory movements are like this: they are inside the soul, ready to be activated, but they only come out when the obstacles holding them back are removed. When they are released, they start to move in the small amount of blood that remains in the sense organs. These movements seem real, just like cloud shapes that quickly change into forms like humans or centaurs. Each movement is a leftover from a real sensory impression, and even after the real impression is gone, the memory of it remains. It's correct to say that, even though it's not really a person like Koriskos, it looks like him. When the person was actually sensing things, their main sense organ didn't call the image Koriskos, but rather, it called the real person "Koriskos." So now, in dreams, the sense organ receives this leftover impression from the sense organs and mistakes it for the real thing. The effect of sleep is so strong that this mistake goes unnoticed. In the same way, if you place a finger under your eyelid, you'll see two images of one object and might even believe there are two objects. But if you know your finger is there, you won't be fooled. The image remains the same, but you don't form the wrong opinion. This is how it works in sleep: if the sleeper realizes they're dreaming and is aware that what they're seeing is just a dream, the image still appears, but a voice inside tells them, "This looks like Koriskos, but the real Koriskos isn't here." Often, while dreaming, people have something in their mind telling them that what they're seeing is just a dream. But if the sleeper doesn't know they're dreaming, there's nothing to contradict the dream.

What I've said is true, and anyone can test it by paying attention to what they experience when they are falling asleep or waking up. Sometimes, just as they wake up, they catch the images that were in their dream and realize they were just movements lingering in the sense organs. Some young people, when it's dark, see lots of phantom shapes moving in front of them, even though their eyes are wide open, and they often cover their heads in fear.

From all this, we can conclude that a dream is a kind of image, and more specifically, one that happens during sleep. The phantom images I mentioned before aren't dreams, nor is anything else a dream if it happens when the senses are fully active. Also, not every image that appears during sleep is a dream. Some people, even while asleep, actually sense sounds, lights, tastes, and touch, though weakly and from a distance. There have been cases where people, while asleep with their eyes partly open, thought they saw the light of a lamp in their dream, and then, when they woke up, realized it was the real light of the lamp. In other cases, people faintly heard the crowing of a rooster or the barking of a dog and then recognized the real sounds once they woke up. Some people even answer questions while they are asleep. It's possible for both waking and sleeping to happen at the same time in different ways. But none of these things should be called dreams. Nor should real thoughts that occur during sleep be called dreams. A true dream is an image based on sensory impressions that happens while sleeping in the strict sense of the word.

Some people never dream in their entire lives, while others start dreaming later in life, having never dreamed before. The reason why some people don't dream seems to be similar to why infants and people who have just eaten don't dream. It makes sense that people who naturally have a lot of vapor rising inside them, which then settles back down, wouldn't have dreams because of the strong internal movement. But it's not surprising that as people get older, they start to dream. As they change with age or emotional experiences, it's inevitable that this shift from not dreaming to dreaming will happen.

• • •

The End

The End

Thank you for Reading

You've Just Read a Piece of the Greatest Library Ever Rebuilt

Thank you for reading.

This book is one of thousands we're restoring, reimagining, and translating as part of the **Modern Library of Alexandria** — a global movement to preserve and share humanity's most important ideas.

What was once lost to fire and time is now rising again — not just as memory, but as living, breathing knowledge, freely accessible to all.

What You Can Do Next:

- **Keep Reading.**

  Discover more legendary works — in beautiful print, audiobook, or digital form — at LibraryofAlexandria.com.

- **Build Your Own Library.**

  Every title is available as a paperback, hardcover, or collectible boxset — at true printing cost. Craft a personal library worthy of display.

- **Spread the Light.**

  Share this book. Tell others about the movement. Help us translate every timeless work into every language, so no reader is ever left behind.

By finishing this book, you've already taken part in something extraordinary.

Join us at LibraryofAlexandria.com

Together, we're rebuilding the greatest library the world has ever known.

With appreciation,
The Modern Library of Alexandria Team

Visit:

www.libraryofalexandria.com

Or scan the code below: